The Ultimate Beginner's Guide to Drop Shipping

How to Get Ready To Start Drop Shipping in a Day

Table of Contents

Introduction

Have you ever wanted to sell products online? This could be great to do when you consider how much money you can get out of the process. There is no limit to the amount of money you can earn by selling products online.

However, the problem with trying to sell items on your own is that it can take more of an effort than necessary to make it work. The process of getting an inventory ready and trying to ship items out to more places can certainly be a burden.

These are real issues that can make it harder for you to start your own online retail store and to make money off of it. However, there's a solution that you can utilize. You can start up you r own drop shipping campaign.

Drop shipping is a simple practice that works with an easy to understand setup. You will get your own website or online store running with a full inventory of products that you want to sale.

These products will come to you through a vendor that you can contact for your drop shipping needs. The vendor will link you to providers that are looking to sell a variety of products and will pay you a good cut of the sale for whatever you want to sell online.

You'll get in touch with a drop shipping provider who will take care of the shipping for you. The payments and orders that you collect will be forwarded to the provider who will then mail out the items for you.

After this, you will get your own cut of the sale. This means that you will get a profit off of the transaction without ever having to handle the inventory yourself. This is an amazing practice but there's more to it than what meets the eye. You will learn many important things about drop shipping in this guide.

The guide will help you to see how you can find a drop shipper and what you need to look for when finding someone to help. After this, you will learn about what you can do to get a website ready to where you can sell the items that you want to offer. The best part about this guide is that you could read it today and get started with your own drop shipping campaign right away on the same time. It's amazing as to how easy this can be to utilize.

Chapter 1 – What Is Drop Shipping?

Drop shipping is a practice that has not been talked about among most people with regards to the ways how you can make money online. However, it just might be one of the best options that you can consider. If anything, it is a very unique practice that is easy to figure out.

Drop shipping is a practice that allows you to make money by selling products to other people. More importantly, it is a practice where you won't have to physically hold any of these products.

What happens here is that instead of buying things and selling them back, you will establish a partnership with a drop shipping supplier. The supplier will allow you to list the merchandise that the entity has for sale.

After you do this, you can collect payments based on what you sell. This can be rather profitable and valuable depending on whatever you get out of the process.

Understanding the Process

Running a business online can be a challenge. However, you can have an easier time making money with your business by working alongside someone else. You can sell someone's products online and make it easier for that party to get items out.

Specifically, you will be working with a separate business that will supply you with items. You will just have to get those items out to the public through your own drop shipping site. As you use this, you will find it to be easy to get your products sold off the right way.

To get a better idea of what happens in the drop shipping process, it helps to take a closer look at how it can call work. Here are the general steps that are used when getting into a drop shipping plan.

1. First, you will acquire inventory from a supplier.

This means that you are going to get in touch with a supplier who will give you access to the inventory. You will have the right to sell that inventory to other people.

The inventory that the other person has will still be in one's warehouse. You will not come in contact with any of these inventory items.

2. The inventory will then be listed through your own website.

You will have the full right to list the inventory that you have acquired through another website. As you will read later in this guide, the types of websites that you can establish can certainly be varied.
Essentially, you are the one who will be marketing whatever the business has to offer. You'll be creating your own page that will give the business you're partnering with a little bit of extra exposure, thus making it easier for products to be sold.

3. You will need to receive a series of proper orders.

The orders that you will take in will include a series of purchase documents. These include details on what people are looking to buy, how they are paying for it, where the product is going to be shipped out to and so forth.
The key here is to forward whatever you get to the supplier. This is to get the transaction to go through.

4. You will then purchase a product after you have taken the payment from the customer.

This step is used to ensure that you will collect money from someone and that you won't be ripped off. That is, you will get the money from a customer and forward it to the supplier, who will then purchase the product for you and send it to the customer.

This is important as it ensures that you won't have to give your own money to the drop shipper. Rather, you will give the money from someone else that is buying the product to the drop shipper. You will still get a part of the sale if the process goes through all the way.

5. The supplier will then ship the product.

After you send the orders and the payments to the supplier, that party will ship the products to the appropriate people who bought them.

6. You will then collect your money.

The amount of money that you can collect varies based on several points like the value of the product you're selling among other contractual terms. You'll have to see what the terms are with regards to whoever you are selling your products to. Either way, you will get a good profit off of whatever you are selling.

The transaction process should be rather simple. It helps you to get the money that you're looking for.

You will learn much more about drop shipping throughout this entire guide. This will help you understand everything that you want to know about how to ship products the right way.

Chapter 2 – What Makes Drop Shipping So Great? (And Are There Problems?)

While what you just read about sounds appealing, you might be thinking a little more about whether or not drop shipping is really a good idea for you to consider. The truth is that drop shipping will certainly be worthwhile as it will provide you with a unique way to make money.

Just look at these great advantages that come with drop shipping and you'll see why it is a practice that you should definitely consider getting into.

Not Much Capital Needed

The problem that often comes with opening your own store online is that you'd have to physically acquire a good amount of capital to sell. This problem will not be a concern if you focus on a drop shipping campaign instead.

You will not have to purchase any products when you get a drop shipping campaign running. Therefore, you will not have to spend loads of money just to get a good store going. You won't have to worry all that much about trying to get it all ready when done right.

It Can Work Anywhere

The fact that this is all done online makes it so you can work on your drop shipping efforts in any place that you are. You can use a drop shipping campaign online and get access to it through a mobile device as well as a traditional computer. Of course, the mobile access that you'll get to your campaign will vary based on where you go to get into a drop shipping campaign.

In addition, you can sell products to anyone in any part of the world. Your venture could offer a full setup where you can sell to people from other countries. You'll have to check with your drop shipper to see if that party can actually support transactions from countries outside your own. Still, those who can do this will certainly expand the overall reach that you will have.

Works For Any Product

Drop shipping can work for just about any kind of product you might find. You can get a drop shipping campaign to sell anything that a provider might stock.

In fact, you can choose whatever products you want to sell on your site through the supplier's stock. The key is to ensure that the supplier has enough of a certain product on hand so you can actually take care of enough orders.

You should be allowed to choose the particular products that you want to sell. This should give you a little more freedom in terms of what you want to sell.

It's Easy To Adjust It On the Fly

Sometimes you might come across cases where you need to change things like the inventory you want to sell, the prices of items and shipping options among other things. You can adjust your drop shipping campaign based on your preferences or what your supplier has on hand. The control will vary based on what the supplier can handle but it will be easy to adjust things no matter what is offered to you.

You Could Earn Anything

There is no limit to the precise amount of money that you can earn on a drop shipping campaign. This allows you to easily sell things and get more money off of them all.

Are There Any Problems?

The benefits of drop shipping outweigh the risks. Still, there are a few things to be aware of:
- There's no real set total as to what shipping costs might be worth. This is due to how a

supplier often deals with many shipping parties.

- There are always times when the supplier might cause an error. This could come from an item that goes missing. This means that while you aren't in control of these things, your supplier still has to be reliable.

- It might be a challenge to see if your drop shipper has enough inventory for all of your shipping needs. You need to check and see if your dropper shipper is suitable.

Overall, a drop shipping campaign could prove to be one of the best things that you might ever get into. It is certainly a great venture to get into as the positive things clearly outnumber any problems that you might come across.

Chapter 3 – Choosing Someone To Do Business With

You might be amazed at the variety of different drop shippers that you can do business with. However, you also have to choose carefully when finding one that is trustworthy and easy to do business with. This chapter is devoted to helping you understand what you need to do when choosing someone that can provide you with the products that you want to sell.

It's true that you can look for different drop shippers through a variety of places. A simple online search can help you out. As much as we'd like to tell you about the various drop shippers that are out there, it would take forever to go through every option.

No matter who you are interested in, you have to take these points into consideration when finding great drop shipper that can help you out.

Experience Is a Must

Check on how experienced a drop shipper is. You should look for one that has been around for at least five years as those are usually the most reliable.

The problem with newer drop shippers is that they might not have established business practices. They might not have enough inventory to sell either. By choosing someone with experience, it will be easier for you to sell things online without any problems.

How Is the Packaging Managed?

A great part of drop shipping is that the provider can offer a custom packaging feature. That is, the packaging will include your enterprise's name and other features on it.

You can even have control over the packaging slips as you can choose to add things like coupon codes or contact information details onto something. You might have to check and see what your drop shipping provider will allow you to print with regards to discounts though.

This will help you show people that you are a reliable party to do business with when finding a great drop shipper. You can show that whatever you have to offer is very easy for anyone to work with.

The physical materials used in the shipping process should not be much of a concern. After all, everyone uses the same cardboard materials these days. The packaging slips should at least show that you put in a huge role in getting a sale to go all the way through.

How Does the Shipping Work?

The shipping process should especially be reviewed with care. This process has to work with a setup where a drop shipper will use a reliable provider to get products out.
A big or reliable shipping company will certainly be essential. You should see that your drop shipper of interest is working with a reliable company like FedEx, UPS or DHL.
National shipping services like the United States Postal Service, the Royal Mail, Canada Post and Australia Post are also worthwhile if you plan on doing business within one particular country.
Don't forget to see if a shipper of interest can handle international shipments. The cost for these shipments will clearly be higher than what you might get for domestic shipping. Also, while many big companies like UPS and FedEx can ship items to multiple countries, it helps to see if a shipper can still support more places. This could help you to expand your international reach over time.

How Are Payments Handled?

The payments that are to be handled by a drop shipper should be checked. It's true that credit and debit cards are popular but at the same time some parties won't take all cards. Some shippers might not accept the American Express or Discover cards, for instance.

Also, some drop shippers can support online wallet services like PayPal. Wire transfers may also work in some cases.

No matter what works, be sure to check and see what payment options can be supported by a drop shipper. The potential clients that you can get to buy things from you will certainly increase in volume when you have more payment options to work with.

Watch For the Charges

While it can be easy for you to get a good amount of money while drop shipping, you have to look carefully in terms of what you might have to pay to your shipper. A drop shipper will typically have a per order fee where you will pay a certain amount of money for the transaction that you are taking in.

The per order fee makes it to where you will still get a percentage of the value of the sale. However, the shipper will collect a good amount of money from the transaction after the sale process is considered.

Watch for any additional fees that might come about through a shipper. A shipper might charge you added participation fees where you will pay a certain amount of money each month to get access to a service.

The membership fee can vary based on who you contact. You might have to pay at least $50 to get started with a drop shipping provider. To make things worse, the membership fee could be charged on a monthly or annual basis. Fortunately, you could get some discounts if you go for an annual basis depending on what you prefer to use.

In addition, you could pay extra for each added supplier that you work with through that same provider.

Restocking fees should also be considered with care. You might have to pay a small percentage of the sale in the event that a product is returned and has to be restocked for whatever reason.

Is a Free Trial Available?

Some drop shippers will provide you with free trials. A trial will allow you to get access to the inventory that you can use for your website or online store.

A trial can help you see what someone has to offer and will help you learn about how to get transactions facilitated. You can use this time to see if a provider is right for your needs.

Be advised that the trial offer will last for a brief time. It can last for a month through most places.

Also, you will be charged for services if you stick around after the trial is over. You will have to cancel your account before the trial ends if you want to avoid paying anything.

Any money that you do make during the trial process will be yours. The same fees associated with what the provider will collect still apply. The only key is that you won't have to pay to get access to the system unless you decide to stick around for a while.

Check the Website

The last tip is to look at the websites of the parties that you are looking to work with. Check to see if the website for someone is presenting enough information on individual products to you. Look and see if the site is transparent enough in terms of how you can sell items, what you can sell and the terms associated with a drop shipping contract.

Be careful when looking around at different drop shippers. It's easy to get into a great campaign if you just look around and see what people have to offer to you.

Chapter 4 – Where Can You Acquire the Right to Sell Products?

You might be surprised at the various types of different drop shippers that you can contact with regards to acquiring the right to sell products from. You will have to look carefully, as you read in the last chapter.

This chapter will focus on some of the many different places that you can visit to acquire different products to sell. There are clearly far too many of these places to choose from but this listing will at least give you a little sampling of the parties that you can work with. You will have to compare each option based on what they can provide you with. Look at each choice to see who has the best solutions so you can find something worthwhile for your overall demands.

Doba

O doba

Doba is a popular website that works with more than 200 different distributors. These groups sell more than two million different name-brand products. Best of all, you can choose different products that you want to sell on your own online store through all of these distributors.

Doba also works with various shopping cart platforms. You can get Doba to integrate with Bigcommerce, Magento and Volusion platforms among many others.

Dropship Direct

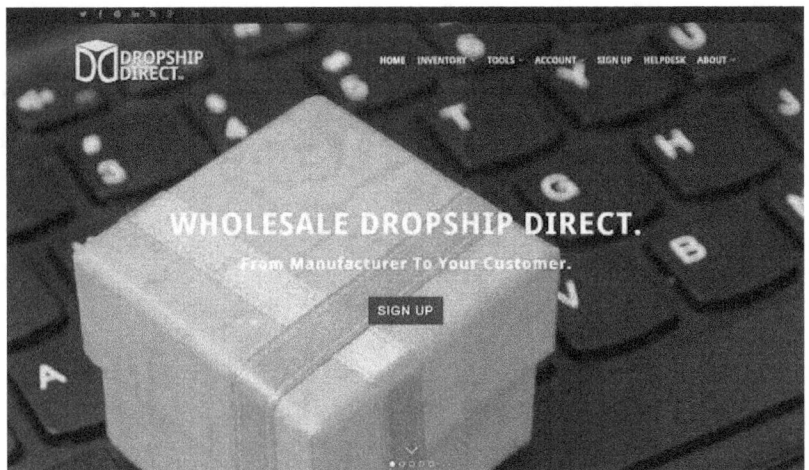

Dropship Direct is a choice that offers more than 120,000 product SKUs in a variety of fields. You can sell health and beauty products, kitchen products, jewelry items and sports fan products licensed by the NFL, the NCAA and many other big-name sports leagues or organizations.

This site works with flat rate shipping charges for most of the products for sale. Automated notifications for shipping processes can also be utilized through Dropship Direct.

Sunrise Wholesale

Your Membership with Sunrise Includes:

Sunrise Wholesale is a provider that can be integrated with an eBay or Amazon online store that you can run. You can choose from 15,000 different brand name products. These products can be sold online through Shopify or Bigcommerce webstores as well.

You can get daily inventory alerts to get a better idea of what you have available for sale as well. Sunrise even offers a setup where you can quickly generate full online listings on eBay or Amazon.

Inventory Source

You can use Inventory Source for your drop shipping needs as well. Inventory Source offers a setup where you can automatically get product details, images and more features loaded to your website or to an eBay or Amazon site. There are more than a hundred suppliers at Inventory Source to choose from but you can also choose to add your own supplier if you prefer. No matter what you choose, you can certainly benefit from the added inventory support that you can come across.

Megagoods

Megagoods has become a big name for how it offers more than a million different products for you to sell through your drop shipping endeavor. You can use Megagoods to get products from various brands sold while also getting your own private labels created. You can customize these private labels in any way that you might see fit. This can add a beautiful look to your website when used right.

There are far too many other choices to look for right now. Just look around and see if you can find options that you know are suitable and attractive for your needs.

Chapter 5 – Where Can You Sell Your Products

After you get in touch with a proper drop shipping provider, you can sell your products. You have to work hard by using a few steps to make it easier for you to get your stuff out there to the public.
Some of these options will allow you to have a little more freedom in terms of what you want to establish. Others will work with proven services that are offered by much larger retail sites. Either way, you should think carefully about where you are going to sell products. It's all about having control and making your products more accessible to everyone.

Your Own Website

You can start by choosing your own particular website. You can set up your own individual website with the use of a store-building software program. Anything that will let you create a unique website will certainly be fun for you to look forward to.

You can use one of many different types of software programs to help you set up an online store. You can use the Coffee Cup Shopping Cart Creator, for instance. This can help you to create a shopping website that you can add your drop shipping items onto.

The assorted types of programs for you to look for can be rather appealing. Either way, you will need to ensure that you have a domain that you can get your site hosted onto.

What's even more is that you can add articles and other long-form bits of content onto your site. You can talk about the products in terms of everything they have to offer and what makes them special. Anything that lets you talk about what you've got to offer will certainly make it easier for you to highlight whatever you've got to sell to someone.

There are many things that must be used if you're going to use your own personal website for your drop shipping needs:

- You must get a domain name to work with. Try and create a domain name that is relevant to whatever you want to sell. You can always go to an online registrar to find domain names that you can use.

- Check the type of program that you have to work with when creating your site. Look to see that it is easy for you to set up something unique.

- Check with your drop shipper of interest. See if the shipper can work with a program and integrate your content.

- Don't forget to look at the type of shopping cart platform that may be used on your site. Whether it entails Magento, Shopify, Squarespace or Volusion among other choices, look to see that the drop shipping process will entail support for that platform.

Open An eBay Site

One of the most popular choices that you can consider when getting your products sold entails the use of an eBay site. eBay has become a reliable place for how it offers an extensive variety of great products.

You can use eBay for your drop shipping needs as many shippers will support eBay pages. They can integrate their operations with eBay pages as needed. In fact, you could have a little more freedom to change prices around on an eBay site. While you will more than likely have to work with a minimum charge for the products, you can always place some items on auction. This could work for high-demand items.

This is a great option for your needs but there are a few important points that have to be explored:

- You will have to get any products that are sold on eBay through a drop shipping process out within 30 days after an order is completed.

- You will still be held responsible for the items that you are selling. This is in spite of how a separate party will ship these out for you. You must keep the terms associated with your shipping campaign under control.

- You will have to work out any problems with a purchase with the buyer. This includes cases where items might not make it to the customer's home within a certain period of time.

- A good template is needed to ensure that you can get a product listed on eBay. Check with your drop shipper to see if that party offers a template that you can use to add information in as well as pictures. This is to make a listing more professional and authentic in its appearance, thus increasing the likelihood of someone to buy a product from your site.

- Be advised that you might have to pay a small fee to eBay for each item that you sell. This could come out of the payment that the drop shipper will give you after a successful transaction is made.

Using Amazon

Amazon is an especially appealing option to consider when trying to work with a drop shipping campaign. This works in that you will get the items that you are selling up onto an Amazon Marketplace page. You will create your own account and then list the items that you want to sell on Amazon through the Marketplace page.

A great drop shipper can support Amazon pages. This can entail the drop shipper taking in the order reports that come into an Amazon page or updating the inventory to ensure that only products that are available for sale are listed on Amazon.

Like with eBay, you must see that your drop shipper can actually support an Amazon transaction. You have to see if a template can be used to help you create a detailed and professional-looking display as well.

These are all good options to think about when you're ready to get your work out online. You can choose any of these great options to help you with getting your work out there while looking more inviting. After all, a good setup can make a real difference when you're trying to highlight your work.

Chapter 6 – Setting Up Your Drop Shipping Account

After you choose the particular drop shipping company that you want to work with and the platform you're going to run, you can easily set up your very own drop shipping account. You might be impressed at how well you can get an account to work for you.

1. Create a proper name for your drop shipping account.

You must start by getting a good name ready for your drop shipping account. You should register your name as a DBA or Doing Business As account. You can go to your local administration office to get your business name registered. This is so you can be legally interpreted as someone who sells products online. This especially makes you more credible.

2. Think about what you want to sell.

As you have already read here, the options for whatever it is you can sell will certainly be amazing and worth checking out. You can choose from a variety of products through all sorts of drop shippers.

Still, you have to think about products based on three factors:

- What you are more interested in selling

- What you know about in general

- Whatever might be in demand based on the first two factors

By using these choices, it can be easy for you to find something that is worth selling.

3. Choose the right drop shipper.

You have already ready about drop shippers and even took a look at a few examples earlier. Think about who you want to work with based on:

- How well the drop shipper can handle your products

- The charges associated with using the drop shipper

- Whether or not your drop shipper can support the particular website or platform that you want to use

- Whether your shipper actually offers the products that you are interested in

- The shipping processes that the drop shipper can utilize; this includes whether or not international support is available

- The types of payment options that can be accepted

4. Acquire a merchant account.

A merchant account can be gathered through your local bank or other financial institution. This can be linked to your website.
This account will be required so you can legally take in other peoples' credit or debit card numbers.
5. See if you can get a PayPal account running.

It should not take long for you to establish a PayPal account so you can take in payments through the popular online wallet service. You must see that your drop shipper can support PayPal payments as well.
6. Create the platform that you will be selling your items through.

You will have to work with one of three options as you read about in the last chapter. You can start your own website, sell things through eBay or sell them through Amazon.
Check on what your supplier can do for you based on the option you choose. Make sure the supplier can give you enough pictures, descriptions and other features to help you with getting your listings to look a little better.
7. Get the listings ready for your products.

The listings that you want to use will certainly vary based on what you want to sell. Check carefully to see what you can get as many of these items out onto your site as soon as you can.

The next two chapters relate to two important parts of the process – what to do if you plan on using your own website and what to do when you actually sell an item.

Chapter 7 - Special Considerations When Hosting Your Own Website

The decision to be a drop shipper through your own personal website can be exciting. You will have more freedom to do what you want with that site when compared with what eBay or Amazon might provide to you.

Still, you have to watch for what you're going to do when getting your own website ready. Here are a few steps that should be followed when getting your drop shipping plan to work through your own website.

1. Choose the right website building program that can help you out.

Check and see that the platform for your website is easy to work with and read. See that your shipper can support the platform too.

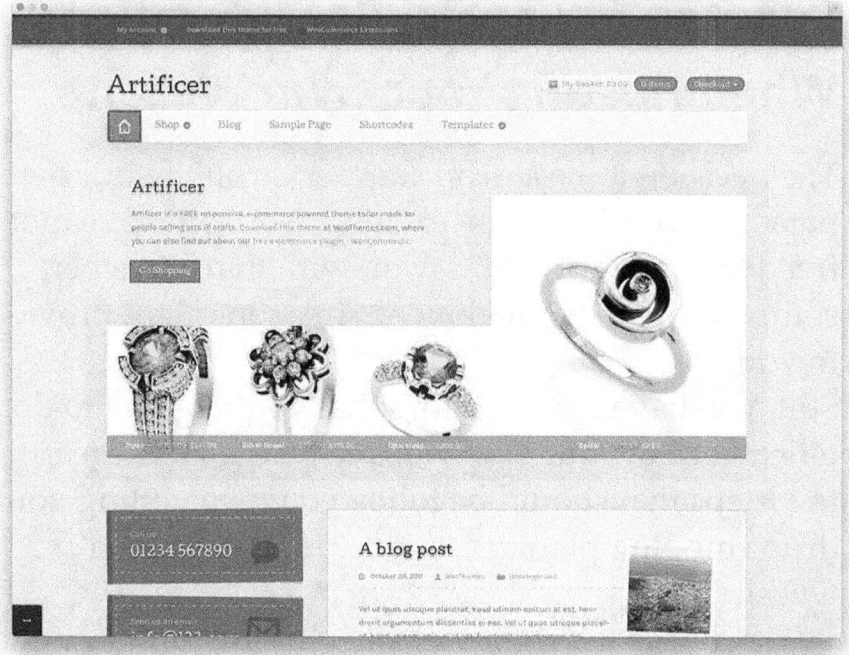

The website you see in the picture above was created by a WordPress-based creator, for instance. This platform is just one of many options that you can use to quickly create your own website.

You must especially see that the website building program can work with an appropriate shopping cart solution. Many plug-ins and widgets can work with different programs that are capable of taking in customers' payment information.

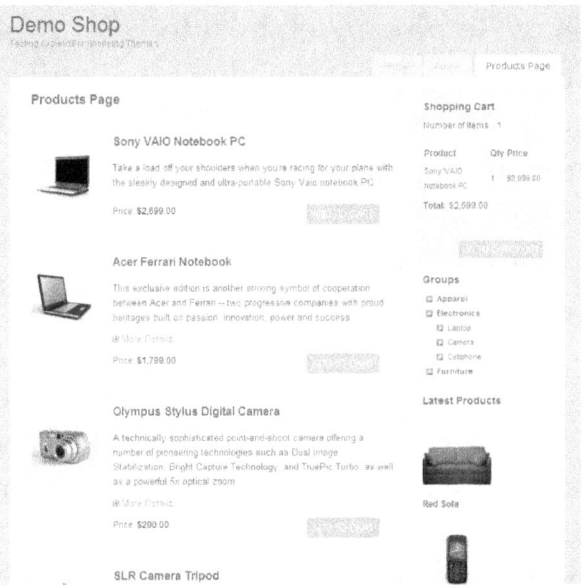

Check with your drop shipper to see what it has to offer. It should not be hard to make your solution work to your advantage when you choose the right option.

   2. Create About and Contact pages on your site.

These will allow people to see what your site is about. They can also learn how to contact you in the event that you need help.

   3. Create a URL for your store.

It should be very easy to find different domain names for your site. Be sure that the one you do choose is relevant to the products or services that you have to offer.

   4. Look for a good web host.

You will have to hire a web host to keep your site online. Check for a great web host that will keep your site online and even offer you with some good website maintenance programs if possible. Don't forget to find a host that will keep your data secure.

5. You must also send out your website to various search engines.

You should submit your website to more search engines, directories and other outside parties. These details must be shared so you can make your website a little more visible.

Like with the URL, the details you send to the search engines should be relevant to the content you've got to work with. Let the search engines know about what you have to offer and use keywords relating to the items you're selling.

The details in this chapter are relevant to those who have created their own websites that can be hosted. Check carefully to see that you are using the right plans for getting your website ready.

Chapter 8 – What Will You Do When Someone Buys Something From You?

You must be certain when someone buy things from your site that you know how to fulfill the transaction. There are many things that have to be done as you are looking to get an order fulfilled the right way.

1. When a person makes an order, get the order details sent out to the drop shipper.

You will have to use the proper integrated features within your website or platform to forward order details to the shipper. The steps for using this will vary by each type of site.

For an eBay or Amazon account, it should not be too hard for you to forward the content to the shipper. For a site that you created on your own, you will have to use the steps listed within your site.

The above picture shows what you can do with a WooCommerce site. You can send notifications out to your shipper to let them know about the purchases that you have facilitated. This will let the shipper know when items have to be shipped out.

2. Check on the shipping and payment processes.

The customer should have specified how the payment is to be made and how the shipping process will work. You will have to send whatever money your customer gave you to the drop shipper. This should be paired with details on the shipping. The money that is being paid for shipping (if applicable) should be included.

3. The supplier will have to be paid a proper total.

The payment will typically entail the wholesale cost involved with the transaction. This means that you will take in a profit based on how much money you sold a product for.

The drop shipper should provide you with the wholesale total after the transaction is fully completed and the product has been shipped to your customer. This is a simple process that should be very easy to use.

Chapter 9 – What Will You Get Paid?

The total amount of money that you will get paid will be influenced by many factors. No matter what happens, you should be paid after the overall transaction has been completed. That is, the drop shipper will have sent the item that you sold to the customer and then get the money in full. The customer should have also received the item that was sold.

Wholesale Versus the Sale Price

There are two points that will make a real difference. First, you have to look at the wholesale value that the drop shipper spends. This refers to the total amount of money that the shipper spent to get the item. Second, you should see what the sale price is. The sale price should be worth more than the wholesale price.

The difference between the wholesale and sale price should be a key factor for what you earn. For instance, if the wholesale price of a product was $150 and you sold it for $225, there should be a $75 profit.

The Charges That the Shipper Uses

Your drop shipper might charge you a certain amount of money on the transaction. This is due to the shipper's need to operate a warehouse, keep a proper inventory and even get shipping plans managed.

Let's go back to the example that you read about a minute ago. The $75 profit might be cut down to $40 or $50 depending on the charges that the shipper might use.

You will still get a good profit. The key is to just look at what someone might be offering to you.

What Other Fees Are There?

Every individual drop shipping provider should be checked carefully based on their fees. Some drop shipping services are going to charge you more than others.

For instance, the membership fee for getting into the service might be high. You could pay $50 to $90 per month as a fee to Doba for use with the total per month being based on the contract. Meanwhile, Sunrise Wholesale charges $30 per month for its services.

You might have to pay extra depending on the number of suppliers you use. Inventory Source will charge $25 to $50 per month for the first supplier and then $15 to $25 per month for each additional supplier that you get after this.

Restocking fees may also apply. This is a fee that the shipper will charge in the event that any merchandise has to be returned. This charge goes for handling the product being returned. Most shippers will charge 15 to 20% of the transaction in the event that this problem comes about.

Remember, there are no limits for how much money you can get out of the drop shipping process. Still, you have to look carefully so you can find a great deal from your shipper.

Conclusion

We hope that this book about drop shipping has helped you to understand everything you need to know about the process. We also hope that you understand everything you have to do to get started. As you start working on your drop shipping campaign, you will start to notice that it is not all that hard for you to get a good practice running. You can find plenty of items to sell online while making loads of money in the process.

No matter what you choose, you must make sure the drop shipping campaign you enter into is organized properly. You have to look to see that your campaign is sensibly prepared and that you've got enough support to work with.

Be sure to look around to see who can help you with getting a great campaign ready. Don't forget to look into how you can find different products that might be of interest for you to sell.

As you go far in your drop shipping campaign, you will notice that you can make as much money as you want out of this. When you do it the right way and prepare well enough, it should be easy for you to get the most out of anything you have to do when making it run.

Good luck with your drop shipping venture!

www.ingramcontent.com/pod-product-compliance
Lightning Source LLC
Chambersburg PA
CBHW070416190526
45169CB00003B/1277